MW01206474

This book belongs to:

....

....

....

BIG STAR
PRESS

Living the Finer Life Journal

Made in the USA
Coppell, TX
24 April 2025

48624886R00066